Grow Your Own Poems

Silver Book Box
Series Editor: Julia Eccleshare

SILVER BOOK BOX

Grow Your Own Poems

Peter Dixon

MACMILLAN
EDUCATION

First published 1988

Published by
MACMILLAN EDUCATION LTD
Houndmills, Basingstoke, Hampshire RG21 2XS
and London
Companies and representatives
throughout the world

Series design Julian Holland
Illustrated by David Thomas

Printed in Hong Kong

British Library Cataloguing in Publication Data
Dixon, Peter, 1937 –
Grow your own poems. – (Silver book box).
I. Title II. Series
821'.914   PR6054.194/
ISBN 0–333–44599–6

CONTENTS

Hello,

Here's a book full of poems for you to read.

If you don't like all the poems, then I hope you'll like looking at the pictures Dave Thomas has drawn.

This is a little bit different from the 'usual' poetry book, because instead of just giving you a poem, I've tried to say a little bit about HOW I came to write the poem.

Poems are not hard to write, anyone can do them . . . and you don't always need special things to write about.

I've written about ordinary things that happened to me when I was at school. Ordinary 'everyday things' like my mum's false teeth. I hope you like them . . .

(the poems, not the teeth!)

A little boy in my wife's class looked at a jar of frog spawn and said:
'Cor – look at that FROGS BORN'.
I think he had the best word.

Frogspawn

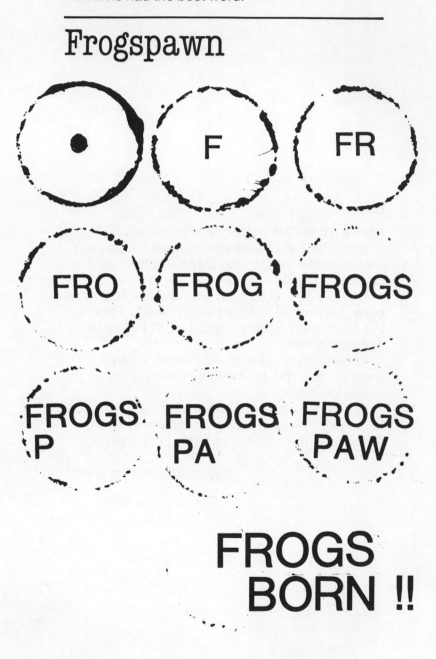

FROGS
BORN !!

I thought up this poem when I was filling the car with petrol. You can invent poems anywhere and any time.

Lost rainbow

One day
coming home from school
(where else?)
I found a rainbow.
Lost
and sad
and torn
and broken
on a garage forecourt.
I picked it up,
wrapped it in a Wonderloaf wrapper
(which was also lost)
and took it home
where I warmed it
and dried it
in front of my mother's fire.
But it died.

I think it must have been
a very old rainbow.

When I was small my mother used to play witches with us. She used to take out her false teeth and hide in the cupboard under the stairs, and jump out. Cupboards under the stairs still seem creepy places.

Playing with witches can be good fun, but you have to be careful!

One day
on a February rainyday –
two small girls . . . playing witches,
accidentally trapped one in the cupboard
                              under the stairs.

The witch screamed,
Beat upon the wall,
And swearing the swear of witches
Tore the gas meter from its iron bracket
– Spat poison through the keyhole,
And flew round the cupboard tearing coats
                              from hooks.

. . .
OUT!
the witch cried –
OUT!
     AND THEN HER FINGERS BEGAN TO COME
. . . slowly at first,
     like carp nuzzling bait
          slowly – under the hardwood door . . .

long
and thin
and strong
and feely!

And they cried . . . and she hissed.
And they wept . . . and she rattled.
And they poured salt on her fingers,
And they stamped on her fingers,
And they beat them with sticks from the shed.
And from the noise and the pain,
The fingers still came,
'til they reached to the catch on the door!

Then out the witch burst!
And she spat and she cursed
From the black
And the dust
And the gasssss . . .
          And she took them away
          For daring to play,
          A game that all children call

My Uncle Bert's ceiling was very cracked, and
when I went to stay with my cousins, we used to
lie in bed 'inventing' pictures in the cracks we
saw. It was good fun, better than television!

The cracked ceiling

Do you remember the ceiling
With its candles and carrots and flowers?
How we lay in the bed, not quite sleeping
And told stories for hours and hours?
Do you remember the witch with white fingers,
The king with a crown on his head,
And the monster with plastercrack features
Who scowled and hung over the bed?
We told every stain of that ceiling,
We knew every mark from the rain,
And how the great grey anaconda
Swung down from the picture hook rail.
We spotted the face of the devil,
We searched for the treasure of God,
And found the whole story of Noah –
And dragons . . . and mermaids . . . and frogs.
The biggest of all was of Hitler,
He stretched from the middle of Spain
To the notch on the centre rose plaster
Then round to the smoke from the train.
But the best of the cracks on our ceiling,
The thing that we all really liked,
Were the dreams that we had in our pillows
. . . After Billy had switched out the light.

I always feel sorry for woodlice. They seem like the poor and unattractive side of animal life. They are dull, grey and boring. I decided to write a poem to make them important and interesting. You can change anything in a poem. You can change the whole world if you want.

Woodlice

Woodlice are lucky
(everyone knows that)
they live in Grandma's cupboard,
and under Grandma's mat.

They live in darkest corners,
they live in woodland ways,
and hide from sun and sunshine
for all their woodlouse days.

Yes – woodlice are magic
(so do them no harm):
just whisper your wishes
as they lie in your palm.

It's lucky to catch one,
they make wishes come true
and the day that you see one –
you'll know what to do . . .

Just whisper your wishes
close in his ear,
and tell him your troubles,
and tell him your fears.

So when you're feeling lonely
and have no friends to play,
or when it's wet and rainy
and you'd like a brighter day –

Then go and find a woodlouse,
and whisper in his ear . . .
he'll listen to your troubles,
and he'll make them disappear.

Actually our dog's not called Kate, because he is a male dog called Reg. Neither does he escape again and again. Poems don't have to be true, though often they start with something that's real.

Kate (the escape)

The day our dog got out
                            again
again
again
was a sad day
a mad day
a bad day.

Kate? ('the escape')

She could gnaw through gas stoves
and wriggle through milk straws!

My dad says she will have to be put down.

But she'll soon climb out.

There are lots of poems I could write about Ben's hamster, particularly the three weeks it spent under the floorboards. What about yours?

The death of Ben's hamster

Gumble died today.

Gumble –
    of whirring wheel
    beaded eye
    and spilt sawdust.

Yes,
Gumble died today
    of one score month and ten.
No more family inquests into who last cleaned
                the cage.
No more gnawings through the nights
and frenzied hours of bedmaking.

For Gumble died today.
    deep
    deep
    deep beneath a treasured world of
                hidden carrot
                blue biscuit
                and sunflower seed.

Just waiting
    waiting
    awaiting the famine
        which never came.

Write poems about things that matter TO YOU: it
mattered to me when our cat got killed in the road.
I don't think I could have written a poem about
anyone else's cat. Just mine!

Marmalade

He's buried in the bushes,
with dockleaves round his grave,
A crimecat desperado
and his name was Marmalade.
He's the cat that caught the pigeon,
that stole the neighbour's meat . . .,
and tore the velvet curtains
and stained the satin seat.
He's the cat that spoilt the laundry,
he's the cat that spilt the stew,
and chased the lady's poodle
and scratched her daughter too.

But –
No more we'll hear his cat-flap,
or scratches at the door,
or see him at the window,
or hear his catnap snore.
So –
Ring his grave with pebbles,
erect a noble sign –
For here lies Mr Marmalade
and Marmalade was MINE.

I always disliked school. I disliked it from the day
I started to the day I left. I still don't like schools
much. When I left for school in the morning I used
to look at the cat and wish I could just lie like him
on the rug all day. I used to wish I could be
anyone or anything that didn't have to go to
school.

Teabag

I'd like to be a teabag,
And stay at home all day
and talk to other teabags
in a teabag sort of way.

I'd love to be a teabag,
And lie in a little box
and never have to wash my face
or change my dirty socks.

I'd like to be a Tetley bag,
An Earl Grey one perhaps,
and doze all day and lie around
with Earl Grey kind of chaps.

I wouldn't have to do a thing,
No homework, jobs or chores –
just lie inside a comfy box
of teabags and their snores.

I wouldn't have to do exams,
I needn't tidy rooms,
or sweep the floor, or feed the cat
or wash up all the spoons.

I wouldn't have to do a thing –
A life of bliss, you see . . .
except that once in all my life

      I'd make a cup of tea.

Questions are easy to ask and I'm
sure everyone could add extra lines
to this poem.

Questions

Do trains get tired of running
And woodworms bored with holes
Are tunnels tired of darkness
And stones of being so old?

Do shadows tire of sunshine
Do tellys tire of fame
And footballs tire of kicking
And puddles tire of rain?

Does water tire of spilling
And fires of being too hot
And smells get tired of smelling
And chickenpox of spots?

I do not know the answers,
I'll ask them all one day . . .
But I get tired of working,
BUT NEVER TIRED OF PLAY.

Remember . . . never push people or this might
happen. And you wouldn't like that . . .
(would you?)

Infant school disaster

Peter pushed past Pauline
and Pauline pushed past Paul
so Peter pushed Paul sideways
then Pauline pushed them all.

Peter knocked the fire bell
and Pauline gave a shout,
the dinner ladies heard them
and they all came running out!

They overturned their custard,
they slipped upon their sprouts
and upset all their puddings
and slipped in coffee grouts.

The shepherds pie went flying,
the pig bins went as well,
then Pauline pushed past Peter
and tried to stop the bell.

The teachers all came running –
they met a sea of stew,
and slipped in all the jelly
(the way that people do).

The teachers all went sprawling
in custard, chips and peas,
. . . jelly on their jackets,
. . . and gravy on their knees.

Miss Morris fell in liver.
Miss Davis in a pie –
one sausage up her nostril
and the other in her eye!

Miss Watson fell in curry,
Miss Jones in mutton fat
and Mrs Ray went sprawling
on a soggy sago mat!

Miss Roberts dived in mango
(and some oriental rice),
then fell on Mr Wilson
(which wasn't very nice).

He yelled for help so loudly
that the Junior teachers heard,
they all came running quickly
(they thought a child was hurt).

Whoosh! went the new Headmaster –
a pork pie in his face,
whilst others slipped and slithered
and skated round the place.

By ones and twos they tumbled,
they stumbled, slid and fell,
whilst Peter, Paul and Pauline
tried to stop the bell.

Oh dear! sighed Paul and Peter,
oh dear! sighed Pauline too,
our teachers told us 'pushing'
was a silly thing to do.

This isn't meant to be a funny poem. It is terribly sad. Fatty Melville went to my school, but I hope children are kinder today than we were. Are they?

Fatty Melville

Fatty Melville
pop out eyes
Fatty Melville
he's got flies
Fatty Melville –
he can't come
snatch his satchel
kick his bum.
Fatty Melville
likes to cry
gobbles sweeties,
cakes and pies.
Fatty Melville one, two, three
Fatty Melville –
can't catch me!
Fatty Melville
smudges ink
'Sit with me?'
'No, you stink!'
Stink like cat sick
all mixed up
with bad school dinner
in a dirty old cup.
Fatty Melville
he can't play
call for us another day
we're climbing trees
but you can't come
we're going to have some thin-boy fun.

So go and eat your cakes and pies
blow your nose and wipe your eyes
you're too fat
you should get thin . . . and if you do
we'll let you in!

23

Teachers seem to think that maths and being able to read and write are the most important things in the whole world. I think there are other things just as important – like dreaming.

Rotten reader

I'm a really rotten reader
the worst in all the class,
the sort of rotten reader
that makes you want to laugh.

I'm last in all the readin' tests,
my score's not on the page
and when I read to teacher
she gets in such a rage.

She says I cannot form my words
She says I can't build up
and that I don't know phonics
– and don't know c-a-t- from k-u-p.

They say that I'm dyslectic
(that's a word they've just found out)
. . . but when I get some plasticine
I know what that's about.

I make these scary monsters
I draw these secret lands
and get my hair all sticky
and paint on all me hands.

I make these super models,
I build these smashing towers
that reach up to the ceiling
and take me hours and hours.

I paint these lovely pictures
in thick green drippy paint
that gets all on the carpet
and makes the cleaners faint.

I build great magic forests,
weave bushes out of string
and paint pink panderellos
and birds that really sing.

I play my world of real believe
I play it every day
and teachers stand and watch me
but don't know what to say.

They give me diagnostic tests,
they try out reading schemes,
but none of them will ever know
the colour of my dreams.

We all know the plural of 'carp' is 'carp' . . . but we always used to say 'carps' . . . so I left it like that. It seems to help the poem.

Carps

There's carps in Boxer's Lake – they said,
With scales as gold as crowns,
With leathered lips, and teeth like chips,
And gills as red as blood.

There's carps in Boxer's Lake – they say,
The big boys told us so –
They're special ones, with eyes like plums
And tongues as long as lies.

They live right in the middle,
They live in deepest mud,
And suck down passing cygnets,
And suck their cygnet blood.

They've been there for a thousand years,
A snorting bubbling brew
Who snap the anglers' fibre rods
And eat the ducklings too.

So – Maurice went to catch one.
I went with him one night,
Along with Kenny Murrell
And Kenny Murrell's bike.

A triple hook with wormcake bait,
Line as strong as wire
And six lead weights, and extra baits
A float as red as fire.

Four hours we stood in Boxer's Lake
Four hours our wellies leaked
And let in nasty squirmy things
That looked like butcher's meat.

We watched our fireglow balsa cork
We watched it still and quiet . . .
A signaller of armies
On a silent summer's night.

The cygnets settled on their nests
They crouched beneath the wing . . .
The evening bat came out to play
The blackbird ceased to sing.

Our wellies filled another inch,
The reedbed creaked its song
And Maurice in his husky voice
Croaked 'Surely, won't be long –'

The crimson float it turned to black,
The water ceased to shine,
And Kenny – in his Kenny way –
Began his Kenny whine.

There's nothing here, there never is
I've never caught a thing.
You won't catch much with fishingline
That looks as thick as string.

So Kenny cycled home, you see
But me and Maurice stayed
And watched the float, and changed the bait,
And watched the shadows go.

That night-time lake filled up with noise,
We heard the sucking carp,
And that is when I had to go,
Before it got too dark.

But Maurice stayed – to catch that fish,
His Mum was never in,
And didn't care about the time,
Or where her boy had been.

So Maurice stayed, and caught that carp.
He caught it dead of night.
A thousand yards of tangled line.
Two hours of frightful fight.

He told me all about that carp
In morning prayers next day,
And how he'd got this massive bite
Just where the cygnets lay.

He told us of its stinking mouth,
Its lips adorned with hooks,
Its fleshy tail, it's evil eye
And fungoid festered looks.

But: I never saw that massive carp
Or saw his cork float fly –
Or saw its withered lumpy lips
Or saw its evil eye.
. . .
He wrote it up in newstime,
He wrote of tangled lines –
And splashing mud, and carpfish blood,
And carpfish howls and whines.

He wrote of shriekings in the lake,
He wrote of carpfish eyes,
And Miss Gardner in her teacher way
Red biroed

See me! Lies!

28

When I was at Primary School I always wondered where teachers lived and what they did. I could never think of them living ordinary lives in ordinary homes. Maybe they don't . . .

Where do all the teachers go?

Where do all the teachers go
When it's 4 o'clock?
Do they live in houses
And do they wash their socks?

Do they wear pyjamas
And do they watch TV?
And do they pick their noses
The same as you and me?

Do they live with other people?
Have they mums and dads?
And were they ever children?
And were they ever bad?

Did they ever, never spell right?
Did they ever makes mistakes?
Were they punished in the corner
If they pinched the chocolate flakes?

Did they ever lose their hymn books?
Did they ever leave their greens?
Did they scribble on the desk tops?
Did they wear old dirty jeans?

I'll follow one back home today
I'll find out what they do
Then I'll put it in a poem
That they can read to you.

I don't like the way schools divide people into
'goods' and 'bads', or 'Prefects' and 'the others'.
This poem tries to say so.

Standards

Oh bring back higher standards –
the pencil and the cane:
if we want education –
then we must have some pain.

Oh, bring back all the gone days
yes, bring back all the past . . .
let's put them all in rows again –
so we can see who's last.

Let's label all the good ones
(the ones like you and me)
and make them into prefects –
like prefects used to be.

We'll put them on the honours board
as honours ought to be,
and write their names in burnished script –
for all the world to see.

We'll have them back in uniform,
we'll have them doff their caps,
and learn what manners really are . . .
for decent kind of chaps!

So let's label all the good ones,
we'll call them 'A's and 'B's –
and we'll parcel up the useless ones
and call them 'C's and 'D's.

We'll even have an 'E' lot!
an 'F' or 'G' maybe!!
so they can know they're useless,
and not as good as me.

For we've got to have the stupid
and we've got to have the poor
because – if we don't have them . . .
well, what are prefects for?

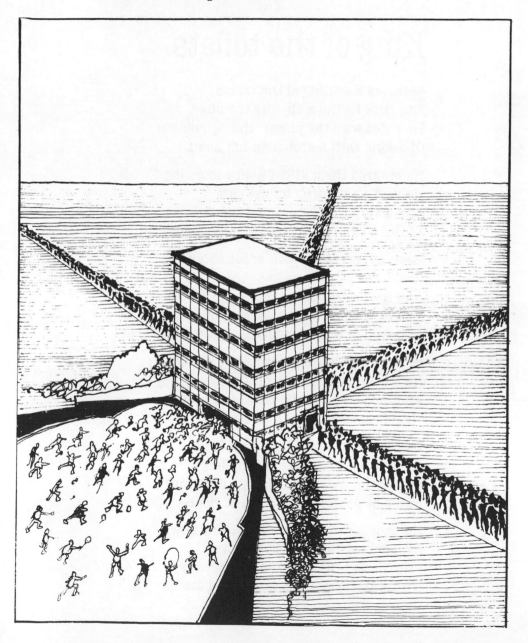

Some children in junior schools like hanging round toilets. Maurice Grimshawe was like that. I was at school with him, and he used to spend nearly all his time playing around in there. It seemed to me that it was the only thing he was any good at!

King of the toilets

Maurice was King of the toilets,
The ones by the wall — by the shed,
He ruled with the power and conviction
Of a king with a crown on his head.

He entered them FIRST every morning
He'd sit on the wall by the gate
And wait for the grumpy schoolkeeper
To unlock them — at twenty past eight.

Then he'd rush in with great shouts of
                                    triumph
And he'd slam all the doors one by one
And he'd climb on the caretaker's cupboards
And he'd pull all the chains just for fun.

He'd swing on the pipes by the cistern,
He'd leap from the top of the doors,
And he'd frighten the new little infants
With bellows and yellings and roars.

He always ate lunch in the toilets,
He'd sit with his food on the floor,
And check who was coming (or going)
And kick at the catch on their door.

He once burst the pipe by the outflow,
By climbing right up on the tank,
And flooded the lower school library,
With water that gushed out and stank.

He once jammed the door on the end one
With five juniors stuck fast inside,
And bombed them with piles of old comics
Whilst they struggled and shouted and cried.

He was useless in class, and at lessons.
He couldn't do hardly a thing –
But when he was out in the toilets,
    THEN MAURICE THE USELESS WAS KING!

I was never any good at French, but I can remember the strange illustrations in our textbooks. Pictures in French books always seem very different from any other kind of drawing. I suppose they are drawn in French. (People were always called Dupont!)

Un jour en France

Un jour –
mon penfriend
en France
discouveré
la première tortue au springtime.
Je trouve la sleepy tortue!
Je trouve ou Toby goes!
exclaime Pierre
et son papa arrive
et mamma arrive
et Les Duponts au next door
les arrive aussi
et les animeaux lovers et tout le monde –
They all came.
. . . et papa dit:
'Ce n'est pas une tortue
c'est un Boche 'elmet!!!'
And he pulled it from the ground.
And then . . .
       and then they saw the soldier
       cocooned in lilac root . . .

Quiet,
and white,
and lonely.
Crusted goggles guarding empty sockets
and lipless mouth grinning its own secret
                                    secret
        like . . .
        where the tortoise really was.

I always admire teachers who take children out for school trips. Especially those who take them to London. School trips are super for kids, but they must be terrible for teachers!

London trip

When we went up to London
The coach was blue and white.
We went all round the Tower
And we saw every sight.

We visited the the V & A
We visited the zoo
We went and watched the Palace Guards
And saw things soldiers do.

When we went up to London
My sandwiches were spam
And Billy Mills had egg and cheese
And 'arny Whitehouse ham.

Johnny Jones had bread and paste
And Maggie Jones had pork
... And when we went to London
Our teacher made us WALK!

We walked all round Trafalgar Square,
We walked all round St. Paul's
And whispered things that didn't work
On whispering gallery walls.

When we went to London
The top came off my drink
It ran all down my trousers –
And made a nasty stink ...

It got all on the coach seats
It trickled on the floor
It trickled on Miss Gardner's bag
And trickled through the door ...

The Science Museum was not too bad –
The toilets there were fun,
We played a game called pull the chain
And slam the door – and run.

We chased around the old steam trains,
We pulled those pully things,
And Martin Knight – he pulled one off
And snapped those bits with springs.

The Albert Hall was really bad,
The Tate was boring too . . .
And that was when poor Enid White
Spilt all her curried stew.

The man in there got really cross
He shouted REALLY LOUD
So everyone came running round
And formed a great big crowd.

Miss Gardner . . . well . . . she sees this crowd,
And smells the curried stew,
And guesses that it's Enid White,
The way that teachers do.

And so – you see – we had to leave
(we'd wiped the pictures clean),
But the journey on the bus back home
Was the best there's ever been!

SEE . . .
Norman brought a pigeon
Back from Trafalgar Square
He said it had a broken wing,
'til it flew up in the air.

It flew all round the driver's cab
It landed in his hair,
It made him wind the window down,
And curse, and yell, and swear.

Miss Gardner – she got really cross,
And made poor Norman cry,
He really thought the bird was hurt
And couldn't hop or fly.

But then we got the punctures.
We got three in a row,
And stuck in Blackwall Tunnel,
While the engine wouldn't go.

We had four smashing breakdowns,
The driver lost his way,
We were five hours late returning
From a really super day!!

. . . .

Three cheers for Miss Gardner and our driver.

Hip . . . Hip . . . . !!!!!!!!!

Seaside towns usually seem full of noisy people who arrive in coaches. They often seem more interested in cafes, amusements and shops than the sea, ships and shoreline.

Day out

They've hidden the great Orange Overlander
with power assisted steering
and overspill ash trays –
behind the portland stone toilets . . .
. . . and it's 50p a time round the only marine
aquarium with a poison sting ray this side of
                                        Bognor.

. . . tap the glass and watch him swim.
. . . the water's bloomin' murky . . .
there he goes!
ugly so and so.
Not worth 50p.
But there's always the live octopus –
that no one can see because he died of
                candy-floss poisoning in 1964 . . .
There's 'is leg
see the suckers . . . cries the man who nearly
                        got left at the Motorway caf . . .
Nasty blighter –
and 53 coach-cricked necks nod in marine
                                        unison,
as the Caribbean Sun Fish
with the tear-stained eyes gazes at the
                        nicotined tapping fingers –
and sadly swims away.
He's another ugly swine, says the man with
        prawn crisps and spittle on his beard,
as they step out into the sun.

If you love someone, you tend to say that you'll do anything for them. You probably want to tell everyone about them as well.

For you

For you
For you I'd like to spray

I LOVE SUSAN

All over
Horse Guards' Parade,
Green Park,
Regent's Park,
The Old Kent Road,
And the wall just round the corner from the
    Tate Gallery.

For you
For you I'd like to pebble-dash St. Paul's
And on every little pebble
I'd like to write

I LOVE SUSAN . . . DAILY.

And then I'd like to wrap it up,
in black silk
of course,
place it in Lovers' Square,
Devizes,
And have the Archbishop of Brighton
    re-name it

ST. SUSAN'S.

Poets always write love poems, but usually they only show them to one person.

When you walk by

When you walk by –
pavements stop playing hopscotch
yellow lines turn pink
and traffic lights turn into something more comfortable.

When you pass by –
buses peer out of bus shelters
lorries turn into lay-bys
and pelican crossings migrate to cooler lands
with pouches full of traffic wardens . . .

When you go by
I watch
from my tower of high hopes . . .
                    and hiding behind a skip full of
memories . . .
by pass . . .
                            on the other side.

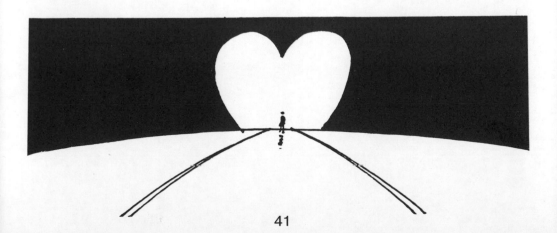

Sometimes you hear a word or a phrase and you can think of another way in which they might be used. The man on the radio kept referring to the 'Turn Off' and it gave me an idea.

Coventry Turnoff

Bernard Burkshaw
who never washed . . .
drove lorries
      up
      and
      down
the M1.
The girls on the coffee urn
at intersection 4
called him
      The Coventry Turnoff.

Read this poem as if you are in the playground picking teams. I wasn't always the last one picked. That was usually Frank Burrows.

Nobody wants a poet in their team

Reds	Blues
We'll have Watson	.......We'll have Piles
Dusty Walters	Norman Eyles
Barney's brother	Porky Day
We'll have Perkins	We've got Ray
We'll have Spaggot	.......We'll have Spud
We'll have 'turnip'	We'll have Cud
We've got Curtis	We've got Mick
We've got Wayne	And you've got Dick
We'll have Sturgiss	.......You have Tone
We've got Robbins	We've got Bones
We've got worst side	You've got best!
You have East	And we'll have West

East is useless   ....Bugs is worse
We'll swap East for Nigel Worth
Come here Worthy, on our side
No! change with Nipper, he's just arrived.

You play this way   ....We'll play that
Three goals change,
   and who
      is that . . .?

        You can have him

Dan's my favourite man, but Arsenal is not my
favourite team, Up The Spurs!!

New signing

A star has signed for Arsenal
(or so the papers say)
a mid-field sort of dynamo
(the man who makes the play).
He's number 5, and 6, and 7,
he ball wins – strikes and shoots
and tackles like an earth machine
in concrete covered boots.
He hacks, and kicks, and shoots, and yells,
he bellows, trips and slides,
and ankle taps and kneecap raps
and many things besides.
He's filled a thousand caution books –
all refs can write *his* name,
and when he comes to Highbury
the game won't be the same!
He'll never pass, he'll spit and roar,
he'll shoot like Al Capone,
a dinosaur of football fields,
a mammoth man of bone.
He cost 2 million pounds, they say,
and I'm his greatest fan.
I'll watch him play on any day

His name is ....

A poet called Roger McGough once came and stayed with us. Late next morning he was still snoozing, and my small daughter peered into his room. She ran downstairs calling 'Daddy! Daddy! There's a poet in the attic!' All I had to do was add the rest of the words.

Daddy!!

There's a poet in our attic
with an ear-ring in his ear
he sleeps the poet's slumber
and his breathing smells of beer.
There's a poet in our attic,
he writes some lovely rhymes —
of merry Mersey ladies,
and murky Mersey times.
He writes it all in booklets
for all the world to read
and tells of wondrous moments
of men's and women's deeds.
He tells it all with passion,
he reads it all with style
and wanders through the country
with a verse for every mile.

There's a poet in our attic
he's the only one we know —
with a belly full of curry
and a memory full of prose.
He's busy dreaming Watchdreams,
he drifts in Mersey miles,
and gathers up the lost words
and places them in files.

There's a poet in our attic
he dreams his dreams of words
and dreams of dreamtime ladies
and dreams of realtime girls.

There's a poet in our attic —
he'll waken when it's day
and write a poet's story
in his poet's dreamtime way.

Charles Causley is a famous poet, and after reading some of his poems about Cornwall I thought I'd try to write something a bit like his . . . only different.

Dear Mr Causley

I'd like to live in Cornwall,
with caves and turqoise seas
and hear the sails of sailors
and feel the salty breeze.
I'd like to live in Cornwall
where wrecks and wreckers are,
and sit and talk with fisherfolk
and sing with jolly tars.
I'd like to get up early,
I'd like to comb the beach,
and find the long lost treasures
that others never reach . . .
     . . . But I really live in Camden Town,
my caves are Wimpey bars,
and I beachcomb on the pavement
and I play in parks for cars.
I never see much fisherfolk,
I never catch a crab,
or watch the seagulls wheeling
or net a sandy dab.
I swim to traffic islands,
I fish in chippy shops,
and never see a dolphin
or shrimp beneath the rocks . . .
     . . . We have no rocks, or weedy pools,
no caverns deep and dark,
no storm strewn shore to wander on
In our tame local park.

My brother though —
outside our house,
finds Chinese meals, all squashy
like seapool things, in silver shells
but squashed by lots of lorries.

We find the screwed up flotsam,
of last night's fish and chips
and like we were in Cornwall
. . . we call them chipwreck chips.

So thank you Mr Causley,
for tales of Cornwall Land
for stories rich as pasties
and golden as the sand.
Thank you for your parakeets,
for sailors sailed away —
and when you come to London Town
we'll take you out to play.

My friend used to live in the same village as the famous painter Stanley Spencer. She told me about how she used to go up and talk to him when he was painting. She was about seven and he was about seventy.

Painter man

Will you paint me in your picture?
I said to a painter man.
Will you paint me in your picture,
Will you paint me if you can?
Will you paint me bright as sunshine,
Will you paint me pink and blue
Will you paint me painter's colours
        like painters always do?

Will you paint me in vermilion,
Will you paint me scarlet hues?
Will you paint in moontime colours
        like painters always do?
Will you paint me lips of ruby
Will you paint me curls of night
        teeth as white as seagulls
        and eyes as bright as light?

Will you paint me in the morning
        amongst the meadow flowers
and in the early evening
        and in the rosetime hours?

Will you paint me when I'm laughing?
Will you paint me when I'm lost —
and in the winter darkness,
and in the autumn frost?

Will you paint me bright and lovely,
Will you paint me in my spring?

    Will you paint me Mr Painter . . .
        I want to hear you sing.

Many poems are about beautiful things, but it is all right to choose 'horrible' subjects. Sometimes it is easier that way.

A very nasty poem

I know a man called Desperate Dan.
I had him home for tea.
I cooked him cow-pie patties,
And he ate 43.
He ate my sister's chocolate.
He ate my brother's gum.
And ate a plate of 'Chappie'
And ate a tin of 'Chum'.
He ate my mother's supper.
He ate her fruit cake, too,
And ate a pound of liver,
And drank a pan of stew.
He started on the freezer
Through pizzas, pies and chops
And even ate some hamster food
And even kitchen slops.
He started on the catmeat
And he'd found my father's beer,
But suddenly went waxen
And whispered 'Dan feels queer!'
I dashed and brought a bucket.
'Not one – get ten!' he cried.
'It must have been the haddock –
I never like things fried.'

People who work in banks always have their names on little notices in front of where they sit. Their names always seem to be very ordinary names. If I worked in a bank I'd like to change my name to something really unusual – just like pop stars do.

Johnny Stardust

My name is Johnny Stardust,
I work in Barclay's Bank.
You'll see my name in letters
On a little shiny plaque.
It was plain Henry Watson
For forty years and more
Until I went and changed it
(Form Deed Poll 904).

I thought of Johnny Demon,
Of Billy Blaze or Dash –
But they didn't really suit me,
They sounded rather flash.
I abandoned Johnny Super
(but kept the Johnny bit)
And joined it up with 'Stardust'
To make a happy fit.
My manager dislikes it,
He huffs and puffs and groans –
He says it 'Isn't Barclays'
Amongst his other moans.
But I like Johnny Stardust,
I think he cuts a dash
. . . And tomorrow, if I want to,
I'll change to Frankie Flash.

I was in the army for two years. I didn't want to be, but I had to be. I am often amused when I see men dress up in army officer uniforms and drill schoolboys who have also dressed up in army uniforms. Once I saw a man 'drilling' just two small boys.

The C.O.
(he's in charge . . .)

On Thursdays, after work,
I put on
Sam Browne,
Gold pips,
Khaki gaiters
(sometimes white),
Blancoed belt
(always tight),
Peaked cap,
Badge
and
Medal.
Then,
With black boots and swagger cane,
Take a bus to 43 Grey's End Road
where
I inspect boys
in
Baggy blouses,
Floppy gaiters,
Saggy belts,
And shrunken hats
on
Short hair heads.
I drill them to defend us against
    Russian TU Aero engined tanks
    Shatter bombs and spatter guns
    Wombats and echo mines

Also
    Egyptian frogmen who swim up rivers
    Or into homesteads via sewage systems
    Disused waterways and Bristol Channels.
I teach them how to run, march, shoot, run,
                     camouflage, and crawl;
    To stand at ease
    To salute me
    (I like that best of all).
So Thursday night is Army night,
The boys are on Parade.
You'll hear us when we march on by,
    You'll hear us when we give our cry . . .
        The boys
           'GET ON PARADE!'
But there are only six.
And last night only two turned up.

I hope you read names on war memorials and realise that they were people's mums and dads, aunties and uncles. Even if you can't feel sad!

Poppies in the park

There were poppies in the park today
with stems of sanded pine
and names like Dick
       and Dad
       and Dave
and words like Passchendaele.
Words like Somme
       Dunkirk
       and Loos
and some more foreign too
some Chinese names like Long Tung Sung
and ones like Sung Hong Soo.
There were crosses in the park today,
all splashed with football mud
with –
THANK YOU UNCLE ARNOLD
and
THANK YOU CORPORAL RUDD.
So 'thank you' Sergeant Fellows
and 'thank you' Enid's dad
for dying for your country –
I wish I could feel sad.

Poets often change things from the absolute truth.
Michael Spurgeon never really existed, but I've
met boys who were a bit like him.

Michael Spurgeon

I remember Michael Spurgeon,
but he won't remember me –
he sat with Maurice Doughty
and he once came home to tea.
He snatched at all the icing buns,
he gobbled all the pies
and ate up all the fairy cakes
and told most awful lies.

I remember Michael Spurgeon
of thirty years gone by –
he played with Billy Simpson
and had a jackdaw's eye.
Fingers quick as silver
tongue as sharp as steel,
lived above the 'Dolphin'
with a mum who wasn't real.

I remember Michael Spurgeon
the worst boy in the street
couldn't do arithmetic
had nasty plimsole feet.
He couldn't draw a picture,
he couldn't catch a ball,
and when it came to reading
– then he was worst of all!

He was worst at all the 'good' things
he was best at all the bad,
and he worked in Tottenham market
with a man he called his dad.
He got caught for selling watches
(they said they weren't his own)
so he had to spend a week or two
in a special sort of home.

But Michael was my best friend
the best at fun and games,
he wasn't scared of teachers,
and he often called them names . . .
I don't know where he lives now.
He's gone, I know not where
with his garden full of children
and his wife with yellow hair.
Perhaps one day I'll meet him,
we'll laugh at times gone by
and I'll watch him drink my whiskey
. . . and wink his jackdaw eye.

Miss Hubbard used to live in the top part of our house. She was really scarey, but it wasn't me who threw gravel at the window. That was Peter Hull.

Miss Hubbard

She's at the window again!
Bug eyed,
Dressing gowned, and grey.
'See her!'
squeal the Brownie pack returning from St. Johns
'See her!'
chorus the boys returning from nowheremuch.
And there she stares –
Tall
and gaunt
and hair unpinned . . .
         staring
         staring
         staring
staring beyond the silver slates
         of Stanley Street
         of Wilmer Way
         and distant Arnos Grove.

Head tilted,
as if by mechanical device
Unmoving,
and unflinching of the handful of gravel
thrown at her window by the captain of the
Boys Brigade . . .
         Always staring.
         Never watching,
         Always staring.
         Staring at her moon.
'Miss Hubbard's moon starin'!' echoed the
         Bunyan boys from 43.

. . . .

And the children gathered
And the pink fingers pointed,
And the gravel rattled.
And still she stared.
And from the houses the grown ups came —
Nodding
And whispering
And pointing . . .

and murmuring wise
things amongst themselves.
To lead the children away.
Later that year they also led Miss Hubbard away.
Slowly
And kindly
For staring at the moon.

Skips of rubbish outside people's homes always interest me. You can tell quite a lot about a family from the things they throw away.

The skip

They're moving out of 24.
Well, she is.
He went a thousand years ago
and the engorged skip with a bellyful of
memories . . . quietly belches possessions
                presents
                and dead cushions
                into the street.
There's breadbins and baskets
there's wardrobes and wheels
there's yesterday's bargains
and yesterday's meals.
There's presents she gave him
there's ones he gave her
from birdcage to mirror
from denim to fur.
It's yesterday's lifetime of being as one.
It's yesterday's lifetime, that sometimes was fun.
But yesterday's lifetime has now gone away
and we live for tomorrow, as you live for today.
A binful of memories squats in our street
for people to sort out their find of the week.
A tipful of gonedays
a tipful of sighs
tipped out in the roadway along with their lies.

Just a binful of memories that people search through.
Just a binful of memories . . .
and they're all about
all about
all about

You

Unfortunately this poem is true.

My best friend

Maurice was bestest at most things,
At spitting and coughing and burps.
He was good at both running and jumping,
And flipping and pulling girls' skirts.
He was goodest at fighting at playtime.
He was fastest at chasing Ron Pugh –
And if ever he came in down your way,
He was bestest at fighting you too!
He was smashing at swearing and yelling,
He was the best in the class at P.E.,
And when it was time for the cowboys
That Maurice was special to see.
He could shriek like a pig at the butcher's
He could shoot from the hip from afar
But when he came round to the dyin'
Then Maurice was really a star!

He began with a roll of the eyeballs
It went to a twitch of the nose,
And slowly he burbled and staggered,
'til he fell like a dead summer rose.
He'd lie on the ground all-a-twitching,
He'd groan and roll into the road,
And stagger around really awful,
And dribble and holler and moan.
He was bestest at dyin' from arrows,

63

He'd pretend he'd been shot in the back
And twist all around on the desk tops,
Like someone being stretched on the rack.
He scared all the infants when dyin'.
They thought that it really was true,
For when you saw Maurice a-groaning
Then you thought that it nearly was too!

He was greatest at everything going.
He was super at mucking about,
And making the teachers get angry,
And making the caretaker shout.
He was bestest at swapping – and marbles
At fibbing and talking in class –
But dyin' is what I remember
For dyin' is what he did best.

He died in the years of his thirties,
No arrows or shots in the back
No staggers
No infants applauding –
No bullets or bombers or flak.

He died quite alone in a side ward.
No stabbings and winning of wars
But a quiet caring nurse and a houseman –
No bellows
Or yellings
Or roars.

His dying I'll always remember.
To us it was always a game . . .
For fighting
And falling
And rolling

   And I wish he had kept it the same.